SRA Open Court Reading

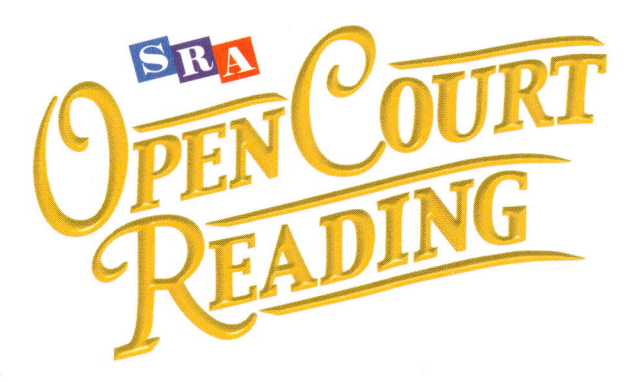

A Stencil and a Pencil

SRA
A Division of The McGraw-Hill Companies

Columbus, Ohio

www.sra4kids.com

SRA/McGraw-Hill
A Division of The **McGraw·Hill** Companies

Copyright © 2002 by SRA/McGraw-Hill.

All rights reserved. Except as permitted under the United States Copyright Act, no part of this publication may be reproduced or distributed in any form or by any means, or stored in a database or retrieval system, without prior written permission from the publisher.

Printed in the United States of America.

Send all inquiries to:
SRA/McGraw-Hill
8787 Orion Place
Columbus, OH 43240-4027

ISBN 0-07-569505-7

3 4 5 6 7 8 9 DBH 05 04 03 02

This is a stencil.

Tom can use a pencil with the stencil.
Tom can make shapes.

Tom can use a pencil with the stencil.
Tom can make a circle.

Tom can use a stencil to make letters.
Tom can use a stencil to print CIRCUS.

Cinnamon can use the stencil.

Cinnamon did not use a pencil with the stencil.

8